*Just like you!*
*W.C.*

# They Chose to be Different
## Unusual California Homes

# They Chose to be Different

## Unusual California Homes

By Chuck Crandall

Chronicle Books/ San Francisco

For Melton Ferris,
and—especially—
for Florence and Irwin Welcher,
good and dear friends

# Contents

# Foreword

The regional character of this book reflects the very nature of the area and its people. Northern California—and particularly the Bay Area—attracts the unconventional, the doers, the trend-setters. In San Francisco *alone* there are more nationally-acclaimed, award-winning residential architects than in any other *state* in the Union. Northern Californians seem to be imbued with the same dare-to-be-different spirit which has made San Francisco everybody's favorite city for over a century. When they build a home, they want more than practicality and shelter—they demand innovation.

Their architects are equally adventurous. Take, for example, the Fresno architect who designed for himself a "hole-in-the-ground" house to prove he could build a habitable shelter for under $15,000, or the Marin County architect who has been building his residence for five years and, with over a quarter of a million dollars already invested, can't stop designing new additions and refinements.

*They Chose to Be Different* is a sampling of outstanding California residential designs north of the Tehachapis. Many of the homes were selected solely because they successfully solved a particular problem, with no consideration of their cost, and a few were chosen to demonstrate that good architectural design can be obtained on a limited budget. But all achieve a definite goal: they serve well the families who live in them. Wherever possible, we show how a family uses its home, and how successfully the architect's design fits each family member's individual lifestyle.

Many of the homes in this book are located on the raw, exposed coastal areas, where the prevalent fog is a damper on nature, where wind is a constant, gruff companion, and where a warm, sunny summer day is a rare luxury. It is illuminating to see how each architect has designed to surmount these obstacles by making the house and outdoor living spaces more pleasant and habitable. Some used atriums and clerestories, others skylights and almost aerodynmically conceived rooflines which channel the wind over the structure.

Other houses are situated in seasonably hot inland valleys, where the glare and heat of the sun can be unbearable. Again, the architects' inventive design solutions—broad hat roofs, wide overhangs, sheltered patios, etc., create enjoyable indoor-outdoor environments.

Vacation homes are no longer A-Frames built from plans snipped out of *Popular Mechanics*. Those who build a second home in the mountains or at the beach now often invest as much in their "getaway place" as in their permanent urban residence. We've included a few of the more provocative examples.

Technical terminology has been kept to a minimum for easy readability and understanding by architectural and design laymen.

# A Family Home with a Workable Plan

ARCHITECT: Marquis and Stoller, AIA
INTERIOR DESIGN: By Owner
PHOTOGRAPHER: Ezra Stoller
LOCATION: San Francisco

An unpretentious exterior hides an exciting interior in this hilltop home. The owners, a family of five, wisely requested that their home fit in architecturally with their neighbors' but they wanted visual drama inside and some separation of adult/adolescent territory. The 3772 square-foot interior is on seven levels, with various living spaces logically related or isolated on separate staggered levels, served by a central stair. Up front is the high-traffic area. Entry from the front, walled play yard is into an informal family room with stairs leading up to the children's domain. Aloof from this area are the adult quarters, study and living room, stacked on different levels in the rear to achieve an adult retreat with controlled access. The stairwell rises from a large interior garden seven levels up to a skylight which can be opened electrically for fresh air. Most major spaces open to the central stairs and benefit from the skylight. Master bedroom and living room have views of the city and the Bay. Materials were kept simple. All interior wood, including ceiling planking and bedroom flooring, is vertical-grain Douglas fir, finished only with clear liquid wax. All walls, except in the kitchen, are white painted gypsum board. Floors in the living, dining, and kitchen levels are unglazed brown Mexican tile, waxed and buffed. Exterior wood is redwood, treated only with bleaching oil.

Modest exterior is misleading. The owners wanted their home to fit with the neighborhood.

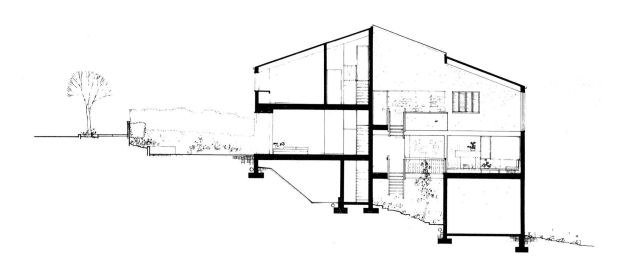

Recessed living area seems cozy, yet open.
Den/study is visible at top of photo.

This view, from the music room, shows three
of the seven levels. Top of photo, skylight is open.

# 2

# Complex Engineering for a Compelling View

ARCHITECT: Frants Albert, AIA
INTERIOR DESIGN: Frants Albert, AIA, and Owner
PHOTOGRAPHER: Gerald Ratto
LOCATION: Seacliff, San Francisco

Almost as interesting as this house is its site, a rocky Seacliff ridge jutting out toward the Golden Gate. The structure could not follow the steep slope, which eventually plunges 100 feet to the beach, so it was anchored to the ridge at the rear and raised at the front on posts. Reaching through unstable sand and clay to rock stratum below are 55 concrete piers spanned by heavy glue-laminated beams carrying joist platforms that cantilever out on all sides. Because the roof would be seen from above, its appearance was important. Changing levels and long, irregular dimensions made a flat roof most desirable, but the roof is usually where mechanical gear and drainage systems are. Drainage was accomplished internally without gutters by creating warped planes over structural surfaces. Stacks and equipment were kept off the roof by placing most vent and duct outlets on west walls, below overhangs. Considerable expense and time were invested by the owners to color-coordinate all materials: Douglas-fir structural wood stained to blend with the redwood elsewhere; fawn-colored gravel for the roofs; a red-gold pile carpet for most floors specially woven to capture the hues in redwood; the reddish-brown stones in the fireplace and hearth. On four levels more or less dictated by the slope of the site, the house consists of a main element containing a small court surrounded by an enclosed walk with access to kitchen, bedrooms, den and dining area; one level up, the bedroom wing; another level up, utility rooms and garage; and on the point of the site the living room, a separate pavilion with an impressive view.

*Steep site posed engineering problems. House faces west with incomparable view of the Golden Gate.*

*Brown quarry floor tile on work surfaces in kitchen are durable, attractive.*

*Atrium/court helps pull light into the interior and is often used for informal dining.*

*Living room has massive stone fireplace repeated in scale and material on exterior wall. The view is an enviable one.*

# 3

# A Module Cluster Approach

ARCHITECT: Jacob Robbins, AIA
INTERIOR DESIGN: By Owner
PHOTOGRAPHER: Morley Baer
LOCATION: Oakland

Here is an innovative solution to the problem every family faces—how does one gain the individual's seclusion without sacrificing the family's feeling of oneness? Architect Robbins accomplished this in his Oakland hilltop home by a two-component system of flat-roofed colonnades and arched vaults which define all spaces. (See drawing.) Each major living space is in its own module set off-axis of the central core, but connected by colonnades to pull the entire structure together visually as a unit. The colonnades are wood-framed with built-up roofs and redwood ceilings. The vaults are self-roofing, self-flashing corrugated sheet steel, arched to span the colonnades. For all floors architect Robbins solved care problems by using radiant-heated concrete seeded with multicolored marble chips rough-ground for a coarse (terrazzo) appearance. Such a floor is impervious to everything from heavy foot traffic to unsaucered plants. The architect broke with tradition again by mixing interior wood types, often in the same room. The kitchen and dining room have redwood lath ceilings and vertical-grain ash cabinets and casework. Exterior woods are cedar with dark-stained redwood trim. Two commendable features of the house are its designed-in provision for future expansion and its sense of privacy—each unit even has a unique view.

*Arched roofs, simulating hills, and natural materials help to make the house part of the landscape.*

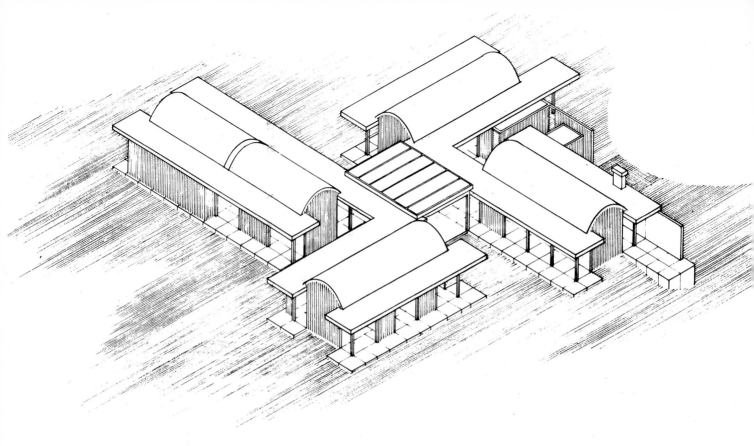

*Main living space. All floors are radiant-heat concrete seeded with multicolored marble chips.*

*Dining room features architect-designed cabinets and lath ceiling. Sliding door, center, opens onto garden court.*

11    A MODULE CLUSTER APPROACH

# 4

# An Eastern Temple in the Oakland Hills

ARCHITECT: Warren Callister
INTERIOR DESIGN: By Owner
PHOTOGRAPHER: Stone & Steccati
LOCATION: Oakland

There is nothing traditional about this home in the scenic Oakland hills. It is totally personalized to the tastes and lifestyle of its owners—an artist-photographer and his wife, a gourmet cook. The site is a pine-studded 12-acre "mini-park" with striking views of Lake Merritt, the Bay, and San Francisco. The architect spent months getting to know the owners before sitting down at the drafting board. Some of his clients' requests and comments were, "We love space. Give us high ceilings"; "We want warmth and simplicity, like a Japanese house"; "Give it an ageless look." The result is a mixture of architectural styles, complemented by the owners' varied tastes in interior furnishings and accessories. Within the 3000 square-foot L-shape are a gourmet kitchen, complete with Chinese oven and cook stove for complicated oriental fare; two dining rooms—one conventional, the other with low table, zabutans, and hibachi for oriental service; and ceilings that soar pagoda-like to frame large windows. To create the desired illusion of age, the pine woodwork was rubbed with two tones of stain and the laminated beams were treated with five coats of color. The upswept roof, the most outstanding exterior feature, rises to 28 feet at the apex. Covered decks the length of the house add to the feeling that the structure might be the retreat of an expatriated Far Eastern religious cult.

*Superb engineering and design have created some unusual structural details and viewpoints.*

*Kitchen, complete with oriental rug, has concrete counters and Chinese oven and cook stove.*

Twelve-acre site is plentiful
with stately pine and cypress.
Abundant skylights provide natural
light throughout the day.

Covered entry frames a charming view
of a traditional oriental garden.

# 5

# A Home among the Trees

ARCHITECT: Edward A. Killingsworth, FAIA
INTERIOR DESIGN: John Hallock
PHOTOGRAPHER: Chuck Crandall
LOCATION: Piedmont

This attractive home in a woodsy section of Piedmont was a design challenge for noted Southern California architect Edward Killingsworth because of a difficult, sharply sloping site. Every tree that could be saved was, and now—seven years later—portions of the house are almost embraced by long, graceful branches. The house is 1900 square feet of simple forms, free-flowing spaces, and large walls broken by expanses of glass. The owners, world travelers and nature-lovers, wanted an open, airy home as well as a setting for sculpture, paintings, and antiques from around the globe. Entry is on two levels—the lower into a small foyer with two bedrooms beyond; the upper into the spacious living room. Judiciously placed floor-to-ceiling windows pour light into the living room from morning until late afternoon and bring the outdoors inside. Dense landscaping and siting provide the seclusion of a mountain retreat, even though the house fronts on a well-traveled city street. No interior structural features impede freedom of movement. This house is eloquent testimony to the wisdom of an "open spaces" design philosophy. Ceilings are high, cabinets and doors extend from floor to ceiling; the dining alcove juts out into the trees and becomes a glass-enclosed patio.

*Difficult, sloping site was a landscaping challenge.*

*Graceful oak branches provide a natural frame for rear of home.*

*Ten-foot ceiling, uninterrupted vertical lines, white walls and an abundance of glass give living room a sense of openness. Note built-in bar, center, which also helps define space. Dining room entry from rear deck is visible at right.*

*Dining alcove gives illusion of being outdoors among the trees. Innovative design eliminated need for heavy structural stress supports around glass sections.*

*Formal entry opens into living room. Stairs lead down to lower-level bedrooms. Den entry is visible at right.*

# 6

# A Private "Museum" in the Berkeley Hills

ARCHITECT: Kaz Shinomiya
INTERIOR DESIGN: By Owner
PHOTOGRAPHER: Jeremiah O. Bragstad
LOCATION: Berkeley

The advantage in knowing your architect well and in having him understand your mode of living is that his design is likely to be precisely what you wanted—as in this case. The site is a steep hillside overlooking San Francisco Bay through a dense grove of eucalyptus trees. At first the owners insisted that *all* the trees be saved, but because that left hardly room to pitch a tent let alone build a house, they compromised and one tree was sacrificed. By placing windows to take advantage of the screening the trees provided, the tri-level 1550 square-foot design captures natural light, provides far-reaching vistas, and closes off the interior from the view of nearby neighbors, so effectively that no drapes are required anywhere, as the clients requested. Young and without children, they required a warm, intimate home for casual living and entertaining, with enough reserve space for a future family. The kitchen, dining, and living areas are in one space, for informal entertaining. And the design is compatible with an extensive collection of 'funk' art and furniture. For an open, uncluttered interior, without an overabundance of furniture, there are many built-ins: dressers in all closets and cabinets and shelves in most rooms. Resawn redwood helps the informality and provides a backdrop for the owners' memorabilia and furniture from the past. The exterior is also resawn cedar plywood. All decks, which seem suspended in the trees, are recessed and have louvered rails which pass light through to the interior but preserve privacy.

*House is virtually engulfed in foliage. Decks, center, have louvers angled to admit light and to screen windows for privacy.*

*Spiral staircase connects the three levels and provides the interior focal point.*

*Master suite has skylight over bed for cloud-watching. Open, unrestricted plan is feasible since only two adults occupy home.*

*Kitchen, dining, and living areas flow into each other to provide a roomy space for entertaining. Master bedroom is in loft above, left.*

# 7

# An Alabaster Palace among the Trees

ARCHITECT: Donald E. Olsen, FAIA
INTERIOR DESIGN: By Owner
PHOTOGRAPHER: Rondal Partridge
LOCATION: Berkeley

The design of this distinctive home (four major awards since completion in 1968) was largely dictated by its site. Architect Olsen says: "Conservation of the giant oaks proved the most demanding problem, not only influencing the shape and disposition of the structure, but also requiring a special foundation method to prevent severing the broadly spreading tree roots." Also, it is an incredible exercise in cost control—about $17 per square foot, or well under $70,000, exlusive of land. Finally, it combines privacy, view, logical floorplan, and novel ideas. The 3700 square-foot home, tucked away on a one-third acre lot separated from the street by a steep canyon and a creek, is accessible only by a 70-foot-long bridge. Two adults and three active boys occupy the home, so a "division of territories" was designed by split-level treatment, with adult and adolescent sleeping quarters on separate levels, and with a penthouse study for an adult retreat. The terrace can be seen through glass walls and reached through sliding glass doors in both the formal dining area and breakfast room. Year-round shade is provided by the magnificent oaks all around. One never loses communion with nature: interior walls and dividers are broken with irregularly shaped windows which direct one's gaze outside. White walls and ceilings contribute to a pervasive feeling of openness and freedom. The owners wanted a home in which to entertain and raise their family without either activity interfering with the other, and they wanted to retain some of the rustic feeling of the site. They got both.

*This aesthetically pleasing front view is a good example of harmony—the architecture complements the elegant oak and vice versa.*

*Spatial relationships are well-illustrated in this photo of the rear. Breakfast room is in center foreground with formal dining room to the left. Bedrooms are in the right wing. Note penthouse above, right.*

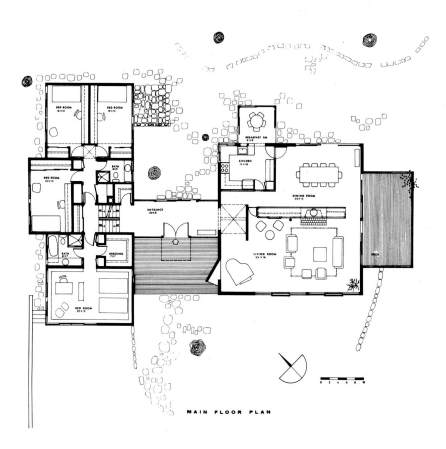

MAIN FLOOR PLAN

*Plan shows how activity areas are logically separated.*

*Open spaces and glass walls create a free-flowing interior. Conveniently placed sliding doors provide immediate access to the outdoors.*

*The formal dining room is awash with light. Built-in cabinets have flush faces finished in white Formica, counters are black Formica. Floors are clear-stained oak strip.*

# 8

# A House Designed for Entertaining

ARCHITECT: Donald Sandy, Jr. Architects & Planners
INTERIOR DESIGN: Jeannette Powell
PHOTOGRAPHER: Joshua Freiwald
LOCATION: Sacramento

The many angles and details of this stark, scaleless exterior make it a pleasure to walk around and observe the subtle play of light and shadow on its complex, energetic, but unfussy design. The lines are sharp and clean, and there are pure white unbroken stucco surfaces, which serve to screen and manipulate shadows, for contrast. Entry is through two large, elegant walnut doors into a highly polished end-grain-block-floor foyer. In the living room, a cathedral-beam ceiling soars to 25 feet at its apex. The house, with a total of 3600 square feet of interior, is ideal for social affairs: noise rises upward and dissipates among the rafters, and there is ample room to circulate. This is what the owners, a socially active couple, wanted: a quiet retreat which can accommodate frequent gatherings of 100 people or more. Most of the ground floor is ''party space'', including the patio and pool, reached by massive 12-foot high sliding glass doors open from the living room onto the patio and pool, where soirees are often held. A stair tower with a large skylight leads to the second level—a mezzanine which overhangs and overlooks the living room. The stair is midway at a bridge between the master suite at one end of the house and a study at the other. In the master suite, level changes distinguish the sitting from the sleeping area and the dressing area from the sunken Roman bath, which has its own skylight.

*Clean lines, exterior devoid of trim.*

*Elevated bedroom has connecting dressing room
and on separate level sunken Roman bath.*

*View from mezzanine shows spatial relationships.
Master suite is at end of hall.*

*Spacious step-down living room seems
even larger with white color scheme.*

# 9

# A Bachelor Home Gives
# Nature a Frame

ARCHITECT: Robert Overstreet, AIA
INTERIOR DESIGN: By Owner
PHOTOGRAPHER: Chuck Crandall
LOCATION: Corte Madera

The architect who designs and builds his own home usually enslaves himself with no time for social affairs or vacation trips, he even filches days from the office. But he never finishes the job to his satisfaction: he is continually modifying and redesigning. However, in its fourth year, virtually all finishing done by the architect himself, an end to Robert Overstreet's project can be seen. Or can it? He selected a remote site in Corte Madera, for its view and rustic environment. The home takes maximum advantage of the terrain, with imaginative windows which become frames for living pastoral "paintings". Clerestories above the livingroom, diningroom and two bedrooms assure comfortable temperatures year-around, let in natural light, and add a feeling of spaciousness. Each of the four main spaces (living, dining and two bedrooms) has its own cantilevered redwood deck accessible through three french doors (a total of 26 french doors throughout—all salvaged from a defunct department store). Most of the house is cantilevered from chemonite-treated poles, and the pole-construction technique is carried through inside. The feeling that the house is a man's is inescapable: natural, exposed wood beams and poles; rough sawn redwood plywood paneling inside and out; massive rusted plate fireplace and hearth, and the absence of feminine influence in furnishings or color schemes.

*Perched high above Corte Madera, the Overstreet home commands a sweeping, unobstructed view of Marin County. Decorative wood detail and trim are repeated inside.*

Dining room, with exposed poles, beams,
and overhead glass-enclosed clerestory,
can be informal (cushions on the floor)
or traditional (architect designed and built
dining table so that legs can be added).
Note built-in wine storage areas
on either side of window seat.

Sunken Roman tub with a woodland view.
Platforms around tub and lavatory tops
are tongue-and-groove teak.
Architect did all installation
and finishing, including tile-setting.

Spacious living room is left open
and uncluttered for traffic flow.
Doorway, right, leads to dining room.

Master bedroom is a picture of spartan
simplicity. Bed is centered in room
and placed on a dais, directly
under a glass-enclosed clerestory.

# 10

# A Glass-and-Steel Gallery/Home

ARCHITECT: Charles P. Stewart, AIA
INTERIOR DESIGN: Charles P. Stewart, AIA
PHOTOGRAPHER: Chuck Crandall
LOCATION: Portola Valley

The architect-owner of this spectacular glass-and-steel home on three oak-studded acres in Portola Valley wanted an uncomplicated design which would not intrude upon the natural environment. He and his wife wanted to enjoy the trees and views, hence sweeping expanses of glass extending from floor to ceiling on all four sides. Space is organized simply, on rigid aesthetic principles: the house is a 60′ × 42′ rectangle, planned on a 4′ 8″ module. Entry is through a gallery-like alcove, flanked by modern sculpture (by a member of the family) and potted plants. Inside, stark white walls are backdrops for more sculpture and paintings. All glass is bronze heat-absorbent and glare-reducing, and each glass wall section can be opened by bronze-anodized aluminum sliding doors. Lights are recessed throughout to preserve the clean, uncluttered interior. For warmth and color contrast, walnut is used in some interior wall panels and doors and on all cabinets. The effect of a pavilion was created by a raised floor slab three feet above ground. Black steel columns support the house and are exposed in the living and family rooms to enhance design continuity. At first sight the house, a radiant, stark crystal structure among the trees, seems out of place in its sylvan setting. But on closer view from inside and out it is seen to be a tour de force in innovative design *and* restraint.

*Front faces morning sun, but bronze glare and heat-resistant glass keeps interior pleasant.*

*Entry, designed as an outdoor gallery, is used to display sculpture, plants, and objets d'art. Subtle lighting yields dramatic effects.*

*Dining and living areas are subtly separated by flooring and furniture. Open space effectively preserves the freedom and openness of the design.*

*Secluded site enabled architect to use abundance of glass for views and natural light.*

# 11

# An Idea House on a Mountain

ARCHITECT: Fisher-Friedman Associates
INTERIOR DESIGN: By Owner
PHOTOGRAPHER: Morley Baer
LOCATION: Alamo

It is easy to see why this hilltop home in Alamo has won design awards. It is fully custom-designed to fit the occupant's lifestyle. Because the owner, a successful graphic designer, splits his working time between his office and his home, he wanted a home studio removed as far as practicable from the noisy sibling disputes of his two sub-teen daughters. The architect's solution was a studio on top of the house, accessible only by a spiral staircase. The owner, also a collector of memorabilia, had acquired a beautiful stained glass window from a razed turn-of-the-century parochial school. His architect worked this into the design as the colorful focal point of the entry. A bowling-alley floor, salvaged from another demolition, is now a durable kitchen floor. Entry is into a gallery foyer which provides an impressive setting for display of the owner's work and collection of art objects. An adjustable lighting system around the perimeter of the ceiling focuses attention on paintings, sculpture, etc. Skylights are spaced to capture light and sun all day long, so that a variety of plants can grow successfully indoors. The foyer floor is easily maintained ceramic tile. The home is an excellent example of how an architect can design for his client's needs.

*Siting will preserve view against future encroachments. Note studio on top of house.*

*Living room is small by most standards, an intimate adult retreat with incomparable views.*

*Entry foyer, loaded with fresh ideas. Stained glass window, a fine example of the art, came from a school. Spiral staircase leads to design studio.*

*Redwood exterior blends well with rustic environment. Decks jut out over steep canyon.*

# 12

# The House That Recycling Built

ARCHITECT: David N. Lynn (Designer)
INTERIOR DESIGN: By Owner
PHOTOGRAPHER: Peter Stackpole
LOCATION: Pleasanton

This delightful residence is what a home should be—exciting, imaginative, and unconventional. All the workmen were free-spirited artist-craftsmen who lived and worked on the 80-acre site for more than a year. The designer, who was also contractor, drew many design details from the skills and talents of his workmen, rather than adhering strictly to initial drawings or concepts—for example, doors were designed and handcrafted on the site. Because the owners wanted to retain the environment, the beauty of which had first captivated them, the house is of forms and materials from nature herself. Rather than cut trees for lumber, timbers and columns from the old San Francisco Hall of Justice were used. Other salvaged materials were railroad trestles; shipyard cargo booms; and planking from temporary Bay Area Rapid Transit construction and from local collapsed barns and fences. Even building stone was collected from the site. The various domes now planted with ground cover, were constructed without forms or balloons by an exterior application of a 1-inch concrete skin, followed by a 1½-inch Gunite interior coat. The plan is roughly semicircular. (See drawing.) The main structure is the primary living area—master bedroom, living room, dressing room, nursery, kitchen and dining room, plus a circular pantry. A covered deck leads to a structure of bedrooms, bath, and playroom. Around the perimeter are four domes—a studio, a kiln studio, a guestroom with bath and sauna, and a garage and underground wine room. Although the 4750 square foot complex was costly ($150,000), it was just the kind of home the owners wanted and provides them with a constant source of enjoyment.

*Partial view of main building. Swimming pool, below, simulates natural pond. Stone used around perimeter came from site.*

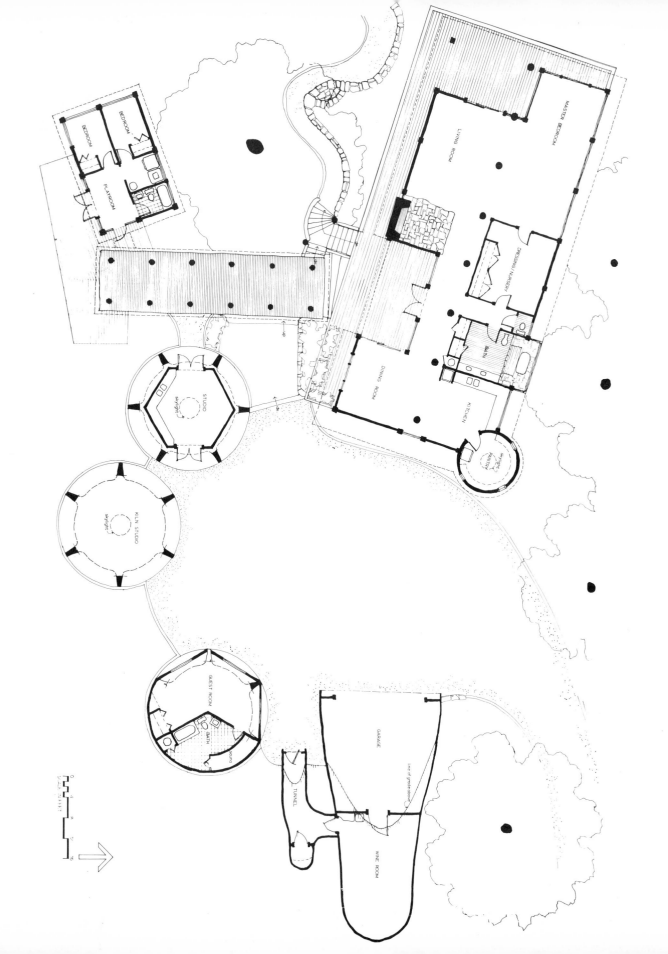

*Domed studio, left, covered walkway, center, and main living wing. Note sod-covered roofs.*

*Garage, left, and guestroom, right. Wine cellar is an underground extension of garage.*

*Main living wing is constructed almost entirely of salvaged materials: floor stones came from site; turned columns and beams came from old San Francisco Hall of Justice.*

# 13

# Living in Tandem

ARCHITECT: Marquis and Stoller
INTERIOR DESIGN: By Owner
PHOTOGRAPHER: Karl Riek
LOCATION: Mill Valley

The site for this award-winning home demanded something unique. Few comparable spots are left in Marin, but the owner acquired an isolated ridge soaring high, with unparalleled views. Marquis and Stoller, one of the country's top residential design firms, created a "Tahitian village" in microcosm for their clients, a young, childless couple who wanted a retreat in which to relax and to pursue their hobbies. Four "houses" or separate elements are connected by a covered walk, each with a pyramidal roof, creating the village-cluster appearance. Since the complex would first be seen from the access road which winds its way down the mountain, the roofscape was carefully considered. The first element is a carport; the second a multi-use space with a ceramic studio and darkroom, occasionally used as a guest room; third is the master bedroom suite; the fourth is the main activity wing, housing the kitchen and dining and living rooms. Although the structure inside and out is of redwood, glass dominates most walls, taking maximum advantage of the view. Without large trees for a natural windbreak, the exposed site required some designed-in protection from the rough seasonal canyon winds and rain: wide overhangs and a redwood retaining wall. Much of the design's appeal is in what *wasn't* done. The temptation to overdesign must have been almost irresistible. The result of the architects' restraint is a very livable house which doesn't overpower its dramatic site.

*Looking like a Polynesian mountain village, this four-element home
has a setting almost unequaled in Northern California.*

*Study alcove was designed by architect, finished by owners. Bookcases, shelving and desks are built-ins.*

*Main living area has one of the few wall spaces not dominated by windows. The view from here is almost a three-quarter circle.*

*Roofscape was conceived as an integral part of the overall design. Shingles are red cedar.*

# 14

# A Simple and Elegant Beginning

ARCHITECT: Charles Moore, AIA
MLTW/Moore Turnbull
INTERIOR DESIGN: Charles Moore, AIA
PHOTOGRAPHER: Morley Baer
LOCATION: Orinda

Is it a pumphouse or an elegant little barn? Neither: it is the first phase of a more ambitious bachelor home in rustic Orinda, designed by and for its architect-owner. But even this tiny (756 sq. ft.) beginning gives a glimpse of a grander plan. The inventive design has won two major awards and has received international exposure. Architect Moore had to design around a county ordinance restricting floor area to a minuscule 700 square feet. Future plans call for a more sumptuous house, complete with swimming pool on his one-acre lot abounding in ferns, bay and oak trees. "To insure against meanness or too small a scale," architect Moore recalled, I bought several 10-foot-long Tuscan columns of solid fir from a San Francisco demolition and decided to design around them." His scheme uses eight columns—four around a skylit pyramidal ceiling which defines the main living space, and four delineating a smaller square with another pyramid above the shower and sunken tub. Getting next to nature and obtaining fresh air on frequent hot days pose no problem for the architect. Sliding doors, either solid or glass, push back on barn-door hardware to expose the interior to the outdoors. Even the front door, a glass panel, slides on tracks. For strength at low cost, the exterior walls are plywood, with cedar shingles for the roof.

*The tiny first increment of an extensive bachelor home.*

Architect used walls creatively to store accessories. Bookcase acts as a divider and privacy screen between two small bedrooms.

Bath with shower and sunken tub seems almost too regal for present structure, but will fit in well when additions are completed. Flooring is brick laid over concrete slab.

Entire walls slide back on tracks for air and unrestricted woodland views.

# 15

# A House on Top of a Mountain

ARCHITECT: Ian Mackinlay, AIA
Mackinlay/Winnacker & Associates
INTERIOR DESIGN: Mackinlay/Winnacker & Associates
PHOTOGRAPHER: Karl H. Riek/Chuck Crandall
LOCATION: Walnut Creek

In designing this award-winning house to sit on a mountaintop over-looking the San Ramon Valley, the architect had four goals: (1) control of the south sun without loss of the view; (2) an inviting entry, especially as seen from the street; (3) room arrangement attractive to most potential buyers (the house was built for speculative sale); and (4) a delicate sense of scale, so that this large (3800 square-foot) house would not overpower its narrow site or the houses to be built on either side. For sun control the house was sited on its lot to take advantage of existing trees; branches were selectively pruned to provide views and to control light penetrating the dining room, kitchen, and master bedroom. The entry was opened up as a part of the hall which links family and guest areas: instead of a blank wall, there is a large window, beyond which is a covered patio/deck, and beyond that a view of the distant hills. For room arrangement the house was divided into zones defined by high roof elements: kitchen, breakfast and dining areas, and a guest bedroom, are in one zone; the master suite is a well-defined and separate zone, yet is not too distant from the children's area. Other spaces are similarly treated. Scale was controlled by breaking the roof up into several elements of related shapes. The relationship of high peaked roofs interconnected by low flat roofs is fully expressed inside. Nature was brought into the plan outside: trees branching out between the roof forms make the house appear to be a cluster of smaller homes.

*Clusters maintain a smaller scale, required by narrow site and future development.*

*Living room with library
behind fireplace. Fireplace is tile with redwood
over sheet-metal firebox and flue, to match ceiling.*

*The three major elements are held together by tiled
deck: which runs through center of the plan.*

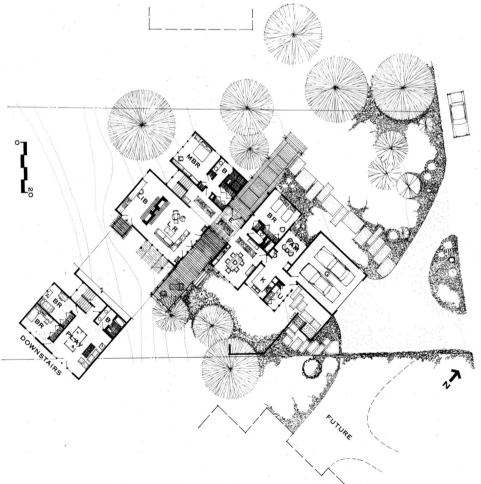

# 16

# A Bold House Over the Water

ARCHITECT: Robert L. Goetz, AIA
INTERIOR DESIGN: Patricia Goetz
PHOTOGRAPHER: Karl H. Riek
LOCATION: Tiburon

A building lot under 85 feet of water? Sounds like a blatant land swindle. On the other hand, why be near the water when you can be *on* it, architect Goetz reasoned. Everything but the entry and garage rests on concrete pilings over the Bay. The two-level redwood Tiburon structure looks as much like an exclusive yacht club as a private residence for a family of five. A roomy deck/boat-dock is anchored to pilings above 200 feet of water; and what seems to be acres of imaginatively designed decks, bridges, and sheltered courts are used in place of patio and back yard. "I wanted a house to make a strong statement—in shape, with vertical emphasis, in its competition with the great mass of water surrounding it," architect Goetz said. "The wood columns, siding, and beams should call to mind the pilings and timbers of its setting." Interior space is roughly 3800 square feet, and every room has a view of the water through entire walls of glass. "Why build a bay or seafront home and be imprisoned in wood and concrete?" architect Goetz asked. "We're fog-watchers. Sometimes it rolls in over the hills toward us and sometimes it's just a finger poking through the Golden Gate." Materials and finish, scale and structural forms all fit well with the site. It achieves what the architect set out to accomplish—a comfortable and casual environment designed specifically for a family's enjoyment of the water and the unique qualities of bayfront living.

*Bayside view shows abundance of windows. Views are of Bay, Sausalito, and the Golden Gate. Bridge at right leads to private deck/boat dock.*

Entry/foyer has ceramic tile floor and serves as a gallery for a portion of the owners' art collection.

Cozy living room has massive fireplace and hearth.

Boat dock/deck sits on pilings over 200 feet of water. Sausalito, in the background, is almost engulfed by fog.

# 17

# A Hidden Jewel on Mount Tam

ARCHITECT: Kenneth Kurtzman
INTERIOR DESIGN: By Owner
PHOTOGRAPHER: Chuck Crandall
LOCATION: Mill Valley

So protected by laurel and redwood trees is this cedar-shingled home on the slopes of Mount Tamalpais that no drapes or window coverings are needed anywhere—just what was wanted by the owners, a young physician and his wife and three children. They enlisted the aid of architect Kurtzman in their search for a site—a wise action, for as a result his design took on a deeper personal involvement. To preserve the site virtually untouched, he left two trees directly in the path to the entry. His floorplan takes into account the decibel range of three active children. Although basically two stories, the house is four split levels served by a central circular stair. Entry is into the top level: a den, a country kitchen, an informal dining area and a formal dining room. Below is a sunken living room open to the level above but sound-proofed by a solid balustrade between them. The third level is the childrens'—three bedrooms, baths, and a playroom under the entry bridge with play deck under the trees. Further down is the master suite. The richly carpeted circular stair is both an effective sound trap between levels and an interior focal point. Large windows (35 feet high) overlooking the Bay to the south provide light and dramatic views all day. There are 2900 square feet of living space inside, and 400 square feet of cantilevered deck. The owners have lived in their home for two years and still find it an "exciting place with a real feeling of comfort and privacy."

*A pleasing mixture of old and new. Arched leaded windows (kitchen) contrast with the strong modern lines of this side elevation. Shingles are cedar, trim is redwood.*

*If one could see through the trees from the road above,
this would be his striking view. The house,
remarkably, was built almost exactly as this "idealized" rendering.
Entry is over bridge, middle right, leading to archway.*

*Spiral staircase leads down to childrens'
level and master suite.*

*Entry bridge is over children's playroom.*

*Sunken living room, with formal dining room beyond.
Balustrade helps buffer noise from kitchen and dining room.*

# 18

# A Tower on The Hill

ARCHITECT: AGORA, Architects & Planners
INTERIOR DESIGN: AGORA
PHOTOGRAPHER: Joshua Freiwald
LOCATION: Mill Valley

It is heartening when a developer turns to an architect for his residential designs, a far cry from the thinking behind, say, the Daly City tracts, or other examples of poor planning throughout the nation. On a beautiful site in the wooded coastal hills that lead to nearby Mt. Tamalpais, the two-tower design seems logical, providing views under, through, and over the trees. Entry is over a short bridge, more an appealing frivolity than a necessity to a central landing between the towers. Primary living spaces are reached by descending a broad stair hall under a great skylight. Living room, dining room and kitchen and connecting decks are on this first level. As one moves upward, the view gets better. On the second level, one tower houses a library/general-purpose room, the other tower the master bedroom with its private deck and view of Richardson Bay. One tower has a third level, a bedroom/study. Although the house is small—only 1400 square feet—even in the smallest room large windows throughout give the sense of space. Tongue-and-groove pine boards, laid vertically and diagonally, also direct one's gaze outward. Redwood and cedar shingles were used on the exterior for easy maintenance and a natural appearance. The architects described the builder's concept thus: "The developers of this house are clearly not appealing to the mass market. . . . they provide individuality and interest, rather than bulk, in a ready-made house. It is a particular process requiring careful site selection and imaginative design."

*Twin-tower house perched on a steep site overlooking scenic valley is a fresh approach to merchant-built development.*

*Living room is bathed in sunlight most of the day. Built-in seating gives more floor space.*

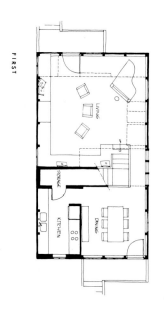

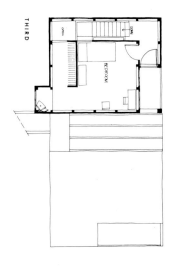

FIRST

SECOND

THIRD

*Skylight extends the full length between the towers. This view is from bedroom level. Living room is on lower level, at left.*

# 19

## A Vacation Home with a Soaring Shape

ARCHITECT: Michel A. Marx, AIA
INTERIOR DESIGN: By Owner
PHOTOGRAPHER: Chuck Crandall
LOCATION: Dollar Point, Tahoe City

Vacation homes should be fun, sprightly, innovative, but, alas, more often than not they are drab and unimaginative. Too many city dwellers take their urban tastes with them to the mountains and lakes. Occasionally, however, some adventurous soul will give his architect free rein, as was done with this charming home on Lake Tahoe's north shore. The owners, a doctor and his wife, wisely gave architect Marx the freedom to design as he saw fit. The result is a delightful, sensitively designed 2700 square-foot structure in perfect harmony with its beautiful setting. There are two levels, plus a mezzanine bedroom (there are five bedrooms in all). The entrance foyer leads into a spacious living-dining area dominated by a huge sail shape glass wall which relates to the design and opens upon a compelling view of Lake Tahoe. The architect sited the house as high as possible on the lot to preserve the lake view above present and future roofs. He also designed a highly original massive stone fireplace and log-storage area which create a cozy family gathering place. All materials inside and out are natural and along with the strong, soaring shapes contribute to a highly successful design.

*Rear elevation shows continuity of design theme. Cedar shingles, when weathered, will help make the structure even less obtrusive in its setting.*

In keeping with the natural, rustic design, the architect created this attractive stone fireplace. Note how he has repeated the structural form of the home in its design.

Strong, soaring lines recreate natural formations and harmonize the structure with its site.

High ceiling opens up the interior for a greater sense of space. Note mezzanine, left, and window area which is boldly integrated into the design.

# 20

# An Hospitable Cave by the Sea

ARCHITECT: Marcel Sedletzky, AIA
INTERIOR DESIGN: By Owner
PHOTOGRAPHER: Robert Singhaus/Chuck Crandall
LOCATION: Carmel Meadows, Carmel County

Too seldom is superlative architectural design combined with reverence for the environment. This magnificent Carmel Bay home designed by Marcel Sedletzky is an excellent example of that rarity. Structural forms are taken from the surroundings. Nature is bold and dominant here with a churning sea and craggy rocks. Completely integrated into the landscape, the house seems to be a rough-hewn outcropping. The garage is half-embedded in the hillside, and most of the roof is overgrown with indigenous ground cover, camouflaging the structure from the road above. The overall effect is the minimal encroachment upon nature that the owners, a nature-loving family, wanted. The five-level interior is entered through a cavern-like passage. An elevator or stairs can be taken to the other levels below. There are eight rooms in all, a total of 3000 square feet. It is immediately apparent that this is not a "cozy" house, by the definition thay many people hold: it is not, for example, paneled and carpeted and padded throughout. But neither is it a "cold" house. Interior and exterior materials are, for the most part, left rough and textured, reflecting with simple honesty the terrain. Walls are reinforced to contrast with the grey concrete. In keeping with the overall design, the fireplaces, of volcanic and Arizona stone, are massive. In essence, the home is a strong, bold architectural statement, but designed with sensitivity. It has the quality of timelessness and should be as fresh and innovative 25 years from now as it is today.

*From the road, the house is almost invisible under its mantle of ground cover.*

Upper left, stairs lead across bridge to entry.

Snug living room has fireplace constructed of Arizona stone and volcanic rock.

The strong textural patterns in the walls
is created from lumber used in concrete
forms. Interesting grain patterns—even
knotholes—are faithfully reproduced.

Massive, fortress-like edifice sits like
a sentinel over Carmel Bay. (Right).

# 21

# Sea-Watcher's Lookout

ARCHITECT: Mark Mills
INTERIOR DESIGN: By Owner
PHOTOGRAPHER: Morley Baer
LOCATION: Carmel

Mark Mills, one of Frank Lloyd Wright's proteges, demonstrates the master's strong and beneficial influence in this fortress-like Carmel home which seems to rise from a churning sea, almost a part of the granite outcropping on which it rests, complementing rather than intruding upon its site. The owners, a mature couple with married children who had lived most of their lives in the intemperate flatlands of Fresno, and during vacation trips were captivated by the rugged coastline and the turbulent sea, told architect Mills, "We want to be as close to the water as safety permits." The compact interior (1700 square feet) uses space with nautical frugality—one bedroom, a small living room, a tiny studio, and a sauna/bath in the main structure, with another 700 square feet of space for the garage and entry ramp. Balustrades or level changes divide the interior. There are no traditional right angles in the house—even the windows and doors are trapezoids. Thick walls are inclined outward to reflect the feeling of the site and to add interior volume. To merge the house with its environment, the concrete was tinted the color of the indigenous succulents. Exteriors were ribbed and bush-hammered to expose the granite aggregate and concrete interior walls were sandblasted for the same texutre. A feature the owners particularly like is that no matter where they sit or stand they are treated to beguiling views of the sea and maritime activity, even a magnificent seascape through a large window in their bedroom.

*House seems to be a natural continuation of the granite ridge. Incoming tides rise almost to the foundation.*

*Cozy living room faces headland, where nature puts on dramatic shows all day.*

*Tiny kitchen and dining area at left call to mind a submarine galley. Living room is at right.*

*Ribbed and textured surface mimics the weathered granite formations nearby. Roof arch is anchored at one end by a roller bearing and at the other by a pin hinge, permitting it to adjust to any gale.*

# 22

# A Get-Away Place at Land's End

ARCHITECT: McCue, Boone, Tomsick, AIA
INTERIOR DESIGN: McCue, Boone, Tomsick, AIA
PHOTOGRAPHER: Jeremiah O. Bragstad
LOCATION: Sea Ranch

Northern California's successful vacation community, Sea Ranch, is typified in this redwood home. Strong on character, whimsical in line, it relates well to its neighbors and, through the use of natural materials to its environment. The goal was a home that is effortless to maintain and provides family members (sometimes as many as 12 at a time) and guests with privacy and seclusion from one another. Both redwood and cedar-shingles on the exterior improve in appearance with age and weathering, so they require no maintenance. Inside, walls and ceiling are redwood. Only indigenous groundcover was used, and nature takes care of that. To achieve privacy, the architects' solution was a plan which consists of two sleeping units flanking a combination kitchen, dining, and lounging area. The adult living space, master bedroom and sitting room, is away from the rest of the house, and the children's quarters are far enough removed so that noise reaches neither the central living room nor the master unit. Although interior living space totals only 2900 square feet, the design creates an illusion of much more room: ceilings soar and plummet at various angles within the same room for a sense of greater space. Walls seem higher because each vertical plank in the redwood paneling is a single piece from floor to ceiling, instead of the traditional butt-joined shorter (and less costly) pieces. Because the site is an exposed peninsula on the coast, just north of San Francisco, some protection from the ocean's strong summer winds was needed; so the exterior is shaped to form a lee. Patio walls provide a windbreak and also create an effective sun-trap. Even on the windiest days, the family gathers here in relative comfort.

*Wood and design forms create visual interest throughout.*

*House is integrated with its spectacular setting, and provides exterior shelter from harsh sea breezes.*

# 23

# The A-Frame Comes of Age

ARCHITECT: Mark Mills
INTERIOR DESIGN: By Owner
PHOTOGRAPHER: Morley Baer
LOCATION: Monte Sereno

Like most of his designs, this Mark Mills residence is highly original. His clients, a plastic surgeon and his family, wanted an A-frame, nowadays something of a cliché in resort cabins. "An A-frame, as such," architect Mills recalled, "seemed too linear for this beautiful site—a wooded hollow which was sympathetic to glass walls with some loft. Heavy tree growth and native vegetation provided natural privacy, so walls of glass without interior draping could be used." He harmonized his sense of the possibilities in the site with his clients' wishes by introducing the A-frame as four gable sides to the square floor plan. The upsweep of the gables allows a 360-degree view outward from the interior, even looking out from the mezzanine. The entire mezzanine, a balcony with a view of the lower level, is the master suite and study. All furniture, except the bed, is built-in and, for the most part, designed by the architect. While the function of the roof framing is, of course, to support weight, here it is also an attractive design feature: two intersecting glue-laminated Douglas-fir arches sweep gracefully across the square plan, with peaked skylight over the central joint. Floors in the ground-level living room, kitchen, sunken "sit pit" and two children's bedrooms are durable grey-green slate. Wood walls and cabinets are tongue-and-groove resawn redwood. Beyond the swimming pool, another building contains a children's play room and doubles as a poolside cabana. Because A-frames usually permit little latitude for inventive design, and creative architects shun unimaginative and overworked concepts, the fact that the architect gave his clients what they wanted, infused with some fresh ideas, makes the house more interesting.

*Cedar-shake arched roof perches on foundation at four points. Structure at right is children's playroom/den.*

*Master suite and study occupy mezzanine level. High gables and balcony treatment allow for adult supervision from upper level, as well as seclusion.*

*Architect's design skill creates visual interest in simple structural forms. Ceiling arches span the interior. View is from living room toward dining area, pool beyond.*

# 24

# A Design to Fit 70 Acres

ARCHITECT: Chris Lee (Designer)
Mark Palmer & Associates
INTERIOR DESIGN: By Owner
PHOTOGRAPHER: Richard Fish
LOCATION: San Juan Bautista

Designer and owner traversed nearly all of the owner's 70-acre estate before finding what they both agreed was the perfect spot, a gorge with tall trees which would provide shelter from San Juan Bautista's seasonal hot spells, and the desired isolation. The design was adapted to the irregularities of the terrain, in keeping with the owner's wishes that the naturalness of the site be undisturbed. The result is a house on many levels with each of the three wings reached by stepping down into a continuous gallery. Not only does this design approach make for a much more exciting interior, it creates a subtle impression of greater spaciousness. Since the client, a busy real-estate broker who deals in large estates and land parcels, needed an office/conference wing, the high-low floor plan effectively separates living quarters and the office area. "Windows became an important factor in the plan," the designer recalled. "It was everyone's goal to get as much light into the interior as possible and open up long vistas across the property. Because the house was designed as three wings, it was feasible to put windows on opposing sides of each wing." Arched windows were used because a traditional touch was felt to be in keeping with the rustic location. Decks and walkways give the various wings a sense of unity, a logical, smooth flow into each other.

*The house is tucked into a naturally landscaped canyon.*

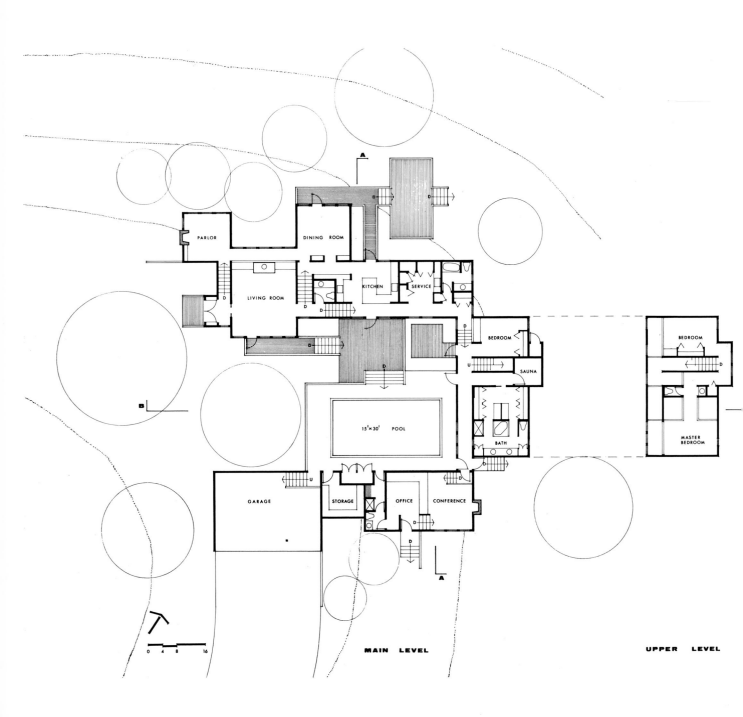

PARLOR

DINING ROOM

LIVING ROOM

KITCHEN

SERVICE

BEDROOM

SAUNA

BATH

15'x30'  POOL

GARAGE

STORAGE

OFFICE

CONFERENCE

BEDROOM

MASTER
BEDROOM

0  4  8  16

MAIN LEVEL

UPPER  LEVEL

*Trees, wisely, were not thought obstructions to building.*
*This one rises through the deck, providing shade and beauty.*

*A desirable kitchen–light, roomy, logically arranged for efficient*
*use. Additional cabinets are hidden under chopping-block top snack table.*

# 25

# A Simple Rock Shelter on the Beach

ARCHITECT: William W. Wurster, FAIA
INTERIOR DESIGN: By Owner
PHOTOGRAPHER: Morley Baer
LOCATION: Garrapata Creek, Carmel

Astute designers know that the natural majesty of the rugged Carmel coast will overpower anything built on it. Internationally esteemed architect William Wurster must have known this instinctively when he saw these craggy, sloping 2½ acres his clients, an architectural photographer and his wife, had the good fortune to acquire. (Scenic shoreline property in this area is seldom affordable). Architect Wurster developed a simple rectangular "box" of granite and glass. "The site is so magnificent and large in scale," he said, "there was no reason to have a complicated structure to compete with it. The simple oblong shape is not fussy, and all the rooms share in the great view." Though outside the house looks traditional, pleasant little surprises throughout add a piquancy both to visual appeal and the living experience of its owners. The open, free-flowing interior is conducive to easy movement and communication. (Only the master suite and bath have doors for necessary privacy.) Level changes alone break up the 2000 square feet of interior. Although a study/library was desired, the owners didn't want to relinquish any of their limited floorspace. The architect solved the dilemna by suspending it from the rafters (the interior is two stories high), with a pass through underneath. The study doubles as a guest bedroom. Windows abound; the best view of the beach, ocean, and rolling hills is from the living room and is appropriately framed in one huge floor-to-ceiling bay window which soars two stories.

*Walls some two feet thick create natural hutches for displaying bric-a-brac.*

*Library/study on balcony takes advantage of high ceiling and requires little floor space.*
*Sunken dining area is underneath, kitchen is at right.*

*Simple, unpretentious structure is beautifully sited below granite outcroppings.*

*View from living room exemplifies the strong appeal of the Carmel coast.*

# 26

# An Artist's Haven by the Sea

ARCHITECT: Mark Mills
INTERIOR DESIGN: By Owner
PHOTOGRAPHER: Morley Baer
LOCATION: Carmel

Carmel Architect Mark Mills' gift for innovative and relevant residential design is evident in this almost futuristic home. His client, a noted artist, wanted to live and work by the sea, "well sheltered from the elements in a structure that has a sculptural feeling." She wanted lots of natural light, like most artists, and views of the rugged, windswept terrain, tide pools, sunsets, and the sea. Architect Mills' solution was a cruciform plan of intersecting barrel vaults with large bay windows at the end of each vault and a dome skylight over the living room. His client wanted all the elements of a masonry structure, but a limited budget ruled out brick or stone. Instead, the architect used the more economical technique of Gunite sprayed three-inches thick over elastomeric webbing. The shell was then coated with a preservative mixture containing rough-ground walnut shells for texture. Another request from his client was that at least one view focus on a tide pool below, so architect Mills angled the study vault downward and gave it a large bay window. There is a rhythm, a symmetry to the structure, clutching lichen-like on the edge of a sheer rock cliff, which delights the eye. It is the kind of house which almost any artist would find stimulating and inspiring.

*House clings, like a giant marine encrustation, to the granite cliff.*

*Intimate study, the owner's favorite spot, overlooks tide pool.*

*Sculptural quality is captured inside, as well. Center entry has custom-designed door with porthole windows.*

# 27

# Excitement Within the Rules

ARCHITECT: MLTW/Moore Turnbull
INTERIOR DESIGN: MLTW/Moore Turnbull
with Ristomatti Ratia
PHOTOGRAPHER: Morley Baer
LOCATION: Pajaro Dunes

Like Sea Ranch, to the north, Pajaro Dunes, a coastal resort community, has rigid design and land-use limitations imposed to preserve an attractive environment. Within a 50-foot square building restriction and a 17-foot height limitation, a redwood home had to be built to accommodate clients, three children, a dog, and weekend guests. Also problems were the harsh glare from the ocean side and the need for privacy from nearby neighbors. The final plan used all buildable land and divided sleeping space between parents and children by a sunny outdoor courtyard between them which is sequestered from wind and neighbors. A large gable roof links both halves of the house. By following the undulations of the sand dunes, additional space was gained inside and out, as well as a more interesting multilevel interior (2090 total square feet). A library and guest space at the entry level are tucked down out of the sun, while the living room rises on a series of wide seat stairs to a sunny vista of the long strand of beach. This center of family activities, made colorful by its blue supergraphics, has access to a decked courtyard. Exposed Douglas-fir interior roof decking, which sets off crisp white walls, is penetrated on the ocean side by a wall-to-wall skylight for abundant natural light to offset the glare of the ocean. The children's bedrooms on the second floor are reached by a skylighted bridge which emphasizes their territorial boundaries. Adventurous sleepers have an aerial deck over the master bedroom reached by a ladder.

*Entry is downgraded, walls are windowless on this side for privacy in this densely inhabited resort area.*

Kitchen/dining area. Recessed
wet bar is behind fireplace.

Terraced deck is used for many activities but primarily
for getting to and from the beach just below.

Decked living room is the result of following topography
of the sand dunes. Fireplace block, adorned with
supergraphics, divides living room
from kitchen and has storage space.

# 28

# A Nautical Retreat

ARCHITECT: Harvey Sanchez, (Designer)
INTERIOR DESIGN: By Owner
PHOTOGRAPHER: Joshua Freiwald
LOCATION: Portugese Beach

This inventive home grew out of a physician's desire for a retreat for himself and his family away from the traditional "escape communities." Since his property overlooked the water, just north of Bodega Bay, he wanted his designer to "do something nautical." The result is a novel living space which captures, in a land-lubber way, some of the flavor of seafaring life. A large central fireplace forms the interior hub. The lower level is a free-flowing space for lounging, reading, or dining. Stairs lead up to sleeping quarters—simple bays radiating off the core, in appearance suggesting crew's quarters on 19th-century square-riggers, complete with rough-hewn planking, portholes that look out to sea, and other maritime details. Since his client's goal was a home where the emphasis would be on casual, unencumbered living, designer Sanchez specified natural materials (primarily redwood) which need little care. Landscaping was limited to low-growing succulents native to the area, to preserve the natural appearance and eliminate groundskeeping.

*Interesting contrast of forms. "Teepee" is main living area . . . shed is two-car garage. Front view is of the Pacific.*

*Sleeping quarters are bays formed by the sloping roof. Authentic ship's bell rousts family and guests for breakfast.*

*Chains, ropes, and beams create a subtle nautical atmosphere.*
*Suspended stair, right, leads up to sleeping lofts.*

# 29

# Lively Design on a Shoestring Budget

ARCHITECT: MLTW/Moore Turnbull
INTERIOR DESIGN: MLTW/Moore Turnbull with Elm City
Electric Light & Sculpture Co.
PHOTOGRAPHER: Morley Baer
LOCATION: Sea Ranch

While some of its neighbors are sleek and palatial, this lively vacation home seems more relevant and comfortable for a casual weekend or a lazy summer. Because the client, a physician with a wife and pre-teen daughters, put most of his vacation-home budget into buying the land, a small grassy meadow on the Sea Ranch coastline, set back from the ocean, an adequate shelter had to be designed within a stringent budget and future development of the area made long-range view protection an important design consideration. "Our solution evolved from the traditional split-level house," the architect said, "with an area close to the ground for accessibility and play, and one high in the air for undisturbed overlook and view." This stretch of coast is frequently cool, and often under a blanket of heavy fog. A central spine scheme brings warmth, light, and color into the center of the house. Family musicians use a tiny minstrel's loft high up in the spine. A vertical bedroom arrangement for the girls economically doubles as a play space with ladder, fireman's pole, colorful graphics, and abstract cutouts. "There is a kind of nautical feeling about the place," the architect said. "The glassy, aerial living room, for example, sweeps the view, much like a ship's bridge. We used studs, plywood, and common redwood boards to build this odyssey of up, down, and around the corner."

*Natural appearance is enhanced by use of common redwood boards.*

*Girls' dormitory/play area. Doors slide on barn-door hardware.*

*Living room was elevated for view over future homes toward Pacific.*

# 30

# A Latter-Day Ranch House

ARCHITECT: D. H. Goltz
INTERIOR DESIGN: By Owner
PHOTOGRAPHER: Gerald Ratto
LOCATION: Sonoma County

This redwood home, calling to mind the ranch houses of the Old West with its large, wrap-around porches and roomy balconies, relates well to its location—the scenic ranch country of Sonoma County. The owners, a recently retired city couple, wanted a home suitable to a slower-paced but active lifestyle. The wife refinishes furniture, restores antiques, braids rugs; the husband pursues a new-found interest in raising horses, for which he needs grazing land. They also wanted two self-contained living spaces on different levels, two houses in one: upstairs a complete floor-plan, including kitchen, and on the ground floor another full unit for visiting children and grandchildren, and guests. As on the early frontier, the kitchen is the family center, for the wife pursues most of her activities there. Although there is adequate central heating, the kitchen has a Franklin stove to create a cozy corner to curl up in on chilly days. The scale of the living room is bolder: its ceiling follows the slopes of the exterior roof and soars 19 feet at one point to meet a skylight. One-by-four vertical redwood siding further accentuates the ceiling height. The large living room fireplace is of native stone from an abandoned winery. Everywhere visual spaciousness has been sought in the sloping planes of the ceiling, the broad entry hall, a five-foot-wide stairway and roomy landing. Wherever practicable, there are long views through the house and out across the hills.

*Decks, wrap-around balconies are outdoor living areas sheltered from the hot sun and inclement weather.*

GARAGE

BATH

BEDROOM
14 x 16

COURT

ENTRY

LIVING ROOM
20 x 20

KITCHEN
10 x 16

BREAKFAST
8 x 16

PORCH

N

## UPPER

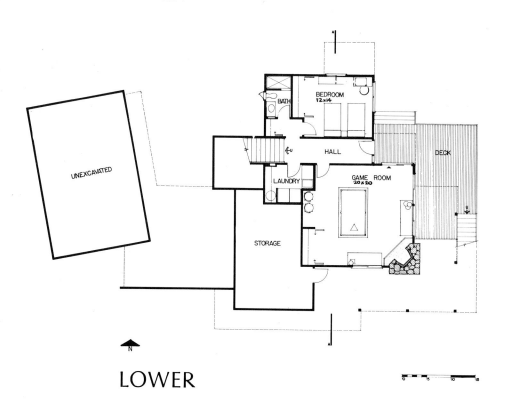

UNEXCAVATED

BATH

BEDROOM
12 x 14

HALL

DECK

LAUNDRY

GAME ROOM
20 x 20

STORAGE

N

## LOWER

*Broad hat roof with wide overhangs helps shield interior from summer sun. Wall between garage and house shields interior and compound for privacy.*

*Redwood surfaces complement owners' collection of antiques and period furniture.*

# 31

# A Cubistic House in a Meadow

ARCHITECT: Burde, Shaw and Associates
INTERIOR DESIGN: Western Contract Furnishers
(Furnishings)
PHOTOGRAPHER: Morley Baer
LOCATION: Carmel

The clean cubistic forms of this multilevel home provide a pleasing sense of balance and mass. The strong, boxy lines are softened by the verdant setting—a 17-acre meadow dense with pines. The owner is a well-known artist and gallery owner in Carmel. He and his wife wanted a modern, functional family-oriented house with many levels and something different on each. The first level houses a well-stocked, temperature-controlled wine cellar—both adults enjoy collecting and sampling a wide variety of California wines. Moving upward, the next level is the family activity room, where the owners, their daughter, and son frequently enjoy chess, pocket billiards, and piano/sing-a-longs. Another level up is the artist's studio, which is more or less sacrosanct. Continuing upward, the next level is the main entry, which is at ground level, then up four steps to the entrance gallery—a room of stark white walls which provide an appropriate backdrop for several of the artist's paintings. Cantilevered decks extending well out and floor-to-ceiling windows throughout preserve the excellent views of Carmel Bay, Point Lobos, and the Pacific Ocean.

*Sculptural quality of the structure is evident in the end elevation.*

*Matched-grain custom-built cabinets separate kitchen and dining room. Doors, center, lead out to deck where family often dines when weather permits.*

*Cantilevered decks make outdoors accessible and open up additional living space on pleasant days.*

*Fire pit is a pleasant departure from the traditional.*

# 32

# A Sky-High Home and Studio

ARCHITECT: James D. Morton, AIA
INTERIOR DESIGN: James D. Morton, AIA
PHOTOGRAPHER: Morley Baer
LOCATION: Squaw Valley

Architect James Morton's forte is the design of mountain residences. As one would expect, when it came time to design a year-round home and studio for himself and his family, the result was superlative. He selected two of the most enchanting acres, on a boulder-strewn, pine-studded plateau a stone's throw from the Truckee River in the Sierra, where he maintains a thriving practice. The site was carved out of the mountain centuries ago by torrents of raging water before the river got its name. As a lover of nature, with a reverence for the natural order of things, architect Morton characteristically chose not to rearrange the terrain to make construction easier. To follow the natural flow of the land, his 3200 square-foot design is somewhat unconventional. And to withstand long, harsh Sierra winters, prime redwood timbers salvaged from the old Yolo Causeway were remilled and polished, then precision cut, pegged, and fitted with Old World craftsmanship. Since both winter and summer the scenery here is so compelling, most of the major living spaces (master bedroom, living room, kitchen, and dining room) jut out from the main structure as separate wings, so that except in the foyer, there is a three-sided exterior view from virtually anywhere inside. The architect's work studio is where one would expect to find it—elevated above the rest of the house with a 360-degree view of the countryside.

*House nestles in the trees on a natural plateau, beside the Truckee River (foreground).*

Living room, like rest of house, has
richly detailed wood beams, framing,
paneling similar to European ski resorts.

Delicate joinery and peg-work, almost a lost art
in this country, is clearly visible in the joists and struts.
View is toward kitchen/dining area wing.

Drift after first seasonal snow
demonstrates need for sturdy roof supports. Severe
Sierra winters dump tons of snow here.

# 33

## Elegant, Economical, Almost Visible

ARCHITECT: L. Gene Zellmer, A.I.A.
INTERIOR DESIGN: By Owner
PHOTOGRAPHER: Douglas Simmonds
LOCATION: Clovis

People laughed when architect Zellmer sat down to design a hole-in-the-ground home. But Gene Zellmer turned a deaf ear to his detractors and forged ahead. "I asked myself, what is the simplest shelter one can build without sophisticated industrialization and new materials, using readily available equipment and materials, and untrained labor? Solution: dig a hole and put a roof over it. Cost? Very low." A tractor dug the hole. The walls follow the natural slope of the earth, in lieu of costly retaining walls. The inner and outer slopes were waterproofed with polyurethane. The rocks inside, set in cement, came from a nearby riverbed. For easy maintenance, a gutter at the base permits hosing down the wall. Columns and beams were built up from 2 × 4s and redwood railroad ties. Floor-covering is indoor-outdoor carpet. Because the berm (earthbank) rises just high enough to screen the neighbors' houses but opens up the treetops and sky views, floor-to-ceiling windows were used wherever practicable. Just beyond the windows are sunken patios. Temperature influenced the decision to go underground: summer temperatures are often well above 100°F, winter occasionally below 28°. On a 112° day at the surface, the temperature 12 inches below is 78°; on a 28° day, a relatively cozy 65°. An above-ground studio/office, reached by ladder, was added. His premise was that a comfortable low cost home could be built, complete with all the civilized amenities, with crude materials and unskilled labor. Cost for the completed home? An incredible $12,000.

*This above-ground view shows office/studio, but gives little indication of what lies below.*

*Built-ins conserve space and money. Seating group bases were fashioned entirely from redwood.*

*Sloping walls are filled with rocks gathered from nearby riverbed, set in concrete.*

*Kitchen has Formica-topped work space, indoor-outdoor carpet.*

# INDEX